SLIPCOVER MAGIC

Edited by

DOROTHEA HALL

~

Slipcovers created by

RON CAROLISSEN

SLIPCOVER MAGIC

Edited by

DOROTHEA HALL

~

Chilton Book Company
Radnor, Pennsylvania

A QUARTO BOOK

Copyright © 1995 Quarto Inc.

ISBN 0-8019-8631-1 (p/b)

This book was designed and produced by
Quarto Inc.
The Old Brewery
6 Blundell Street
London N7 9BH, UK

Editor Laura Washburn
Art Editor Julie Francis
Designer Debbie Mole
Illustrator Elsa Godfrey
Photographer Paul Forrester
Picture Researchers Jo Carlill,
Susannah Jayes
Art Director Moira Clinch
Editorial Director Sophie Collins

Typeset in Great Britain by
Genesis Typesetting, Rochester
Manufactured by
Regent Publishing Services Ltd,
Hong Kong
Printed by
Leefung Asco Printers Ltd, China

CONTENTS

FABRIC FACTS

DON'T GET completely carried away by a fabric's design before you have also considered its suitability for the job you intend it to do. First check what it is made of, how well it will wear, how easy it will be to clean and if it is safe to use.

Decorator fabric fibers

Decorator fabrics are made from a wide range of fibers that fall into two main categories.

Natural fibers Wool, linen, cotton and silk are resistant to dirt and clean well. However they can shrink when washed and cotton, linen and silk may crease.

Man-made fibers There are two types of man-made fibers: those derived from natural materials but treated with chemicals and those that are totally synthetic. Rayon and viscose are made from regenerated plant material which has been chemically treated. They are unlikely to shrink, but are less resistant to wear than synthetics.

Synthetic fibers Acrylic, nylon and polyester, amongst others, are usually stronger than natural fibers. They are crease resistant, mothproof and usually shrink proof. However the fibers attract dirt and so a synthetic fabric needs more frequent washing. Many fabrics are made up of a mix of natural and man-made fibers so that the benefits of each may be combined.

Fabric options

Choose a tough, hard wearing fabric that is closely woven for slipcovers as they take a lot of hard wear. Linen blend, a mixture of linen and cotton, is the traditional choice but medium weight cotton, ticking or a tough cotton and polyester mix are all suitable. Avoid very thick fabrics as these are difficult to sew, especially if you include piping in the seams. Large designs can look very effective but bear in mind they take accurate positioning and there is likely to be a lot of waste when you center the design. Also think about aftercare of your fabric. Machine washable fabrics are easier to live with but you will be limited in your choice as most decorator fabrics require dry cleaning.

Shopping for fabric

Before you buy fabric check that it has no flaws and that the design has been printed on to it straight. As you need to cut lengths across the grain accurately a design that is askew can cause real problems. Buy too much

Think about the suitability of fabric for the task at hand.

Fabric can be indoors or outdoors, practical or whimsical.

There are many factors to consider when choosing your fabric. Consider the use of your cover: will it be indoors or outdoors, or both, and will it need to be changed with the seasons. The fabric on this chair is a good example of a practical, all-around choice.

rather than too little fabric as it is important it all comes from the same batch number. This means that it has been printed at the same time so the color will be the same throughout. A later batch can come up slightly different. Some cheap fabrics may have been bulked out with a finishing to look of better quality than they really are. When washed the finish disappears to leave a thin, limp material. Rub the fabric to check for a finishing.

Hall chairs, or other items that are ornamental, can be covered in any fabric, even lace, and the effect is stunning.

QUESTIONS TO ASK BEFORE YOU BUY FABRIC

1 Will it wear well?
Slipcovers and chair seat cushions take a lot of wear and need to be made from tough fabrics if they are to last.

2 Will it clean easily?
Check that washable fabrics will not shrink or wash before you use them but be aware that they may continue to shrink to some degree. Cushion covers will probably need more regular cleaning. Slipcovers and upholstery fabrics gain from having a stain resistant finish. Some fabrics have already been treated or treatment may be available.

3 Will it look good?
Fabrics used for gathered or pleated furnishings need to drape well. Check this before buying. Check that sofa and cushion cover fabrics will not crease. Crumple them in your hand then watch to see if the creases quickly disappear when you release them.

4 Is it safe to use?
It is important to use flame-resistant fabrics on sofas and chairs. Look for the label or ask in the shop.

5 Will it be exposed to bright light?
Strong sunlight fades fabrics quickly, especially is you choose bright colors. Look for fade-proof fabrics.

6 What style do I want to create?
The elements of any room will look most effective if they have style as a unifying factor. Pick a style you like; country cottage, farmhouse, formal, period, minimal or whatever then keep fabrics, flooring, furniture and wall decoration to the same theme.

Let fabric work for you to create rooms that are both beautiful and comfortable.

CREATING WITH COLOR

COLOR IS the most obvious and exciting element in a room and for this reason it is easy to be fearful of making a mistake when creating a color scheme. However it is not difficult to put colors together that complement and enhance each other, and the room where they appear, if you follow a few simple ground rules. The most interesting homes are those that highlight the characters of the inhabitants, so start by collecting samples of color combinations that please you.

Combine neutral tones with fabric pattern and texture.

Absence of color can also be an effective basis for an interior decor scheme and slip-covers, which can be removed for easy washing, are ideal for a white fabric.

Using neutrals

Apart from true colors, dealt with in the color wheel, there are the neutrals, those shades which contain no color. These are black, white and grey. Beige and all its tones – cream, mushroom, off-white, fawn, stone, sand, tan and so on – are usually referred to as neutrals too. A neutral is often used as the basis for a restrained scheme, then small splashes of color are added to provide interest. Neutrals can also be used together very effectively to create a rustic, natural look. This is most successful where a wide range of textures is also included.

The color wheel shows how colors work together and against each other to achieve the desired effect.

Contrast colors are those that work best together.

Putting colors together

It is easiest to work with color if you start by using a color wheel. The color wheel, like a rainbow, is made up of red, orange, yellow, green, blue and violet. Each of these colors is interspersed by the color which is a mixture of the two on either side of it. Using tones of one color, known as a monochromatic scheme, can be very effective, but choose the tones carefully. A yellow-green will not look good beside a blue-green. To ensure success pick tones from the same side of the true color. So mix blue-greens only with other blue-greens or yellow-greens with other yellow-greens. Closely related colors, that is colors which lie next to each other on the color wheel, are considered harmonious when used together and provide a background that is easy to live with. A harmonious color scheme could include sand and terracotta, or lavender and pink, or denim blue and aqua. However a scheme made up totally of tones of one color or of harmonious colors can be bland. Contrasting colors (known in the trade confusingly as complementary) lie on the opposite side of the color wheel and a contrast color can be used very effectively to enhance the main color. The contrast is best used in small amounts as color accents. Imagine a green sofa piped in red or aqua pillows displayed on an apricot-colored covered chair. Look at fabric designs and you will see how often a small amount of a contrast color has been introduced and how well this accent color shows off the main shades and lifts the whole design.

Blue adds a cool tone as well as a restful atmosphere to rooms in which it is used.

Hot and cold colors affect our feelings about a fabric.

Hot and cold colors

By looking at the color wheel you can also see that colors fall into one of two categories, warm or cool. Those on one side of the wheel, red, orange and yellow, are warm colors while those on the opposite side – green, blue and violet – are cool colors. This allows you to create a feeling of warmth in a sunless north-facing room by using a warm color or, alternatively, to provide a cool atmosphere by using blue, green or violet tones in sunny south-facing rooms where you want to create a restful effect. Remember, too, that warm colors are stimulating whereas cool colors are relaxing.

Yellow warms up a room and adds a lively note to the decor.

Effect of color on space

Cool colors appear to recede from you, warm colors to come towards you. Therefore a room decorated in cool colors will appear more spacious than one decorated in warm colors, which will look more cozy. However the strength of color you use will also have an effect on this feeling of space. Light tones, or tints in which a little color has been added to white, will also make a room appear spacious. A room's dimensions can be changed visually by clever use of color in other ways. A high ceiling will appear lower if it is painted in a deeper tone of the wall color. A light-colored floor covering will also make a room appear larger, as will low furniture that matches the floor covering in color. A cornice rail or chair rail painted in a dark color will diminish the sense of space. Make a hall, or long, narrow room appear shorter by painting side walls and doors in a light tone, end walls and doors in a deeper tone.

Successful color matching

Few people are able to carry colors accurately in their minds. It is much wiser to take samples of chosen paint colors, fabric swatches and furniture tones with you when you go to choose other items for a room. If you do not have a sample then match the color up to a length of embroidery silk or a spool of sewing thread and take this instead. Always bring home samples of alternative choices before you buy. Pin all the samples – fabric, paint, wallcovering, carpet and so on – to a board and leave this in the room where the scheme is to be used for a few days. View the samples in both day and artificial light. This is important as lighting changes colors dramatically.

CHOOSING COLORS – SEVEN POINTS TO BEAR IN MIND

1 Where do I start?
Few people have the chance to decorate a room from scratch. Consider all the points below if you have this opportunity. Otherwise consider existing colors or patterns when choosing additions.

2 Which exposure?
Bring sun to a north facing room with warm colors: yellow, apricot, red or pink. In a sunny south-facing room where you want a cool, sophisticated effect go for blue, lilac or green.

3 Do I want the room to appear larger or more cozy?
Cool colors or pale tones used on all the surfaces will make the room appear more spacious. Warm colors will provide a cozy look, strong shades will create a dramatic effect.

4 Is the area used over long periods or just passed through?
Frequently used rooms are generally best decorated in pale, easy to live with and restful tones. Use more exciting and brighter color schemes for halls, landings, bathrooms or spare rooms.

5 Is the room cluttered with furniture and accessories or simply furnished?
A room already busy with bits and pieces looks best with a plain one-color or neutral background. If you aim for a minimalist look a simply furnished room can also benefit if walls, flooring and furniture are kept to the same color. Alternatively provide splashes of bright accent color to give a simply furnished room interest.

6 Is it a room used mainly in the day or more at night?
Colors can look very different in daylight and artificial light so make sure you check your choice at the time when the room is in most constant use. In a brightly lit room the same color will also appear less intense than in a dark room.

7 Can I be sure the color I choose from a paint chart will look the same on the wall?
No! Because colors on a paint chart are usually surrounded by a border of white they appear paler than they really are. A good tip, if you have any doubts, is to go for the shade slightly lighter than the one you originally picked.

PATTERN AND TEXTURE

TOGETHER WITH color, the choice of pattern and of texture are important elements in creating a room's character. Like color they can make a room feel cozy or give it a spacious feeling.

The effects of pattern

Pattern creates an illusion of depth in a room. Small patterns appear to recede and therefore create a feeling of space in the same way that cool colors do. So use small patterns to make a small room larger. In a large room unless the design is very bold they fade into insignificance. Bold patterns, which like warm colors appear to come towards you, are best kept for large expanses of window, wall or floor and are ideal for slipcovers, especially if the color is strong. In a small space choose pale colors or they can easily be overpowering. If you want to use a large design in a small room consider using it in shades with plain curtains at the window or wallpaper that goes up to chair-rail height, then use plain paint or a textured paint finish above. Alternatively pick a bold design for matching slipcovers and curtains then use plain toning color for the walls and floorcovering. Pattern is a wonderful aid to changing a room's dimensions visually. Horizontal stripes will increase the apparent length of a wall, or use a picture or chair rail to create the effect. Vertical stripes will make a low ceiling appear higher. Widen a room with flooring in a pattern that runs across rather than along the room.

Placing a large motif in a central position on your cover makes for a stunning effect.

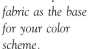

Choose a patterned fabric as the base for your color scheme.

Planning with pattern

The simplest way to create a color scheme is first to choose a fabric and then pick out colors from the design for plain walls and flooring, shades and accessories. Re-introduce the pattern in small items like seat cushions, throw pillows, lampshades or use it for piping.

Putting patterns together

The wide range of coordinated papers and fabrics provide many mix and match opportunities. To be sure of success use color as the linking factor. If color matches you can successfully mix geometric and floral patterns. For instance choose a bold floral fabric for curtains then pick out one of the colors from the fabric for striped wallpaper and the same color to make slip covers from checked fabric.

Use texture to add or diminish warmth in your interior.

Texture

Texture appeals to our sense of touch as well as sight. A surface may be rough or smooth, shiny or matt and these elements are tactile. They also work visually, like color and pattern, to create space or to diminish it, to make a room appear cool or cozy. Shiny surfaces, such as satin and glazed fabrics for instance, reflect light to create a feeling of space. But shiny surfaces are also cold looking and too many can feel unfriendly. On the other hand textures that are rough, or soft with a matt finish such as wool, tweed and velvet, absorb light and provide a more cozy look. Although the effect is warm and comfortable, again, too much can also be claustrophobic. The most effective way to use texture is to mix shiny and matt, smooth and rough, hard and soft.

Texture adds substance and drama to what could be an otherwise ordinary fabric.

GETTING THE MOST FROM PATTERNS AND TEXTURES

• Use pattern, like color, to change the apparent shape of a room. To make a small room apear more spacious use mini-prints. Two-color or two-tone paint effects also provide subtle pattern and texture.

• Texture changes color, appearing much brighter on shiny surfaces, more muted or richer on matt surfaces. Use shiny surfaces to attract the eye to features you want to emphasize, and matt finishes to play down unattractive features.

• Tone down a too boldly patterned room with the introduction of sheer fabrics at the window. These filter the light entering the room and soften colors.

• Extend the use of texture to the display of accessories. Break up the hard outline of a lamp base or picture with a feathery-leaved plant.

BEFORE
YOU BEGIN

Sewing your own slipcover is a truly rewarding experience, one which will give years of pleasure and fill you with pride, but there are certain steps that must be taken before you begin. This chapter covers the basics of slipcover making, from start to finish, and will help to clarify the fine points of slipcover sewing.

9 Mark the seamline on the outside back (B), rounding the corners to fit the chair. Pipe the lower edge and clean finish the piping ends. Baste the ties as marked.

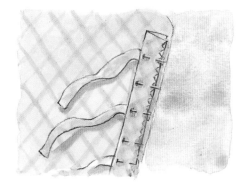

10 Make up facings to clean finish the back edges of the side openings, which should end level with the last tie. Fold the fabric sections (G) in half lengthwise and pin to each side, right sides together. Stitch, catching the ties.

11 Pin and baste the outside back to the inside back, right sides together. Stitch along the top edge only, using the zipper foot and stitching close to the piping.

12 The skirt is made in two parts: the back (the width from back leg to back leg) and the front (from one back leg around the front to the other back leg). Join the skirt pieces (E) for the front skirt along the short edges. Hem the side openings and bottom edge. Stitch two rows of gathering threads along the top edge. Pull up the gathers evenly to fit the lower edge of the gusset.

13 Pin the main skirt to the lower edge of the gusset with the right sides together, then stitch around through all layers. Trim and clean finish the raw edges. Repeat on the back section, making sure the edges of the skirt are equal at the side opening.

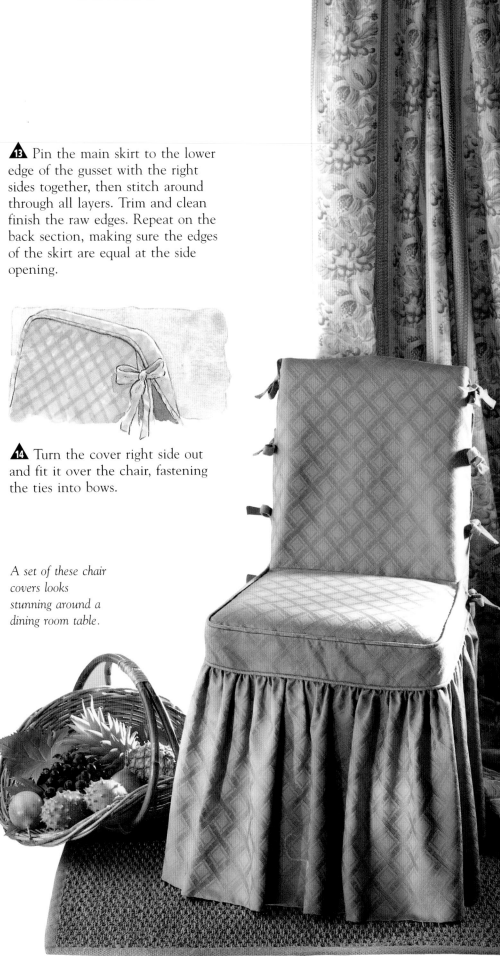

14 Turn the cover right side out and fit it over the chair, fastening the ties into bows.

A set of these chair covers looks stunning around a dining room table.

TWO-PIECE CHAIR COVER

This cover is designed for upright chairs with upholstered seats.

CHECKLIST

Materials

closely woven decorator fabric
medium-weight polyester batting
paper for pattern
general sewing equipment   pages 110–11

Techniques

piping and binding   pages 118–19
using batting   pages 122–25

Measuring up

To the following measurements, add ⅝ inch seam allowances:
Inside and outside back – Measure length and width; allow two pieces (A).
Seat cover – Measure the width and depth; allow two pieces (B). Make a paper pattern for the shape, see step 2.
Binding – Allow enough fabric for the perimeter of the back and seat covers, with a depth of about 2 inches (C).
Ties – Allow for ten pairs of ties (D), ours measure 2 inches wide and 10 inches long.

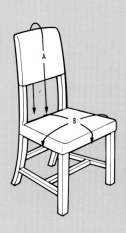

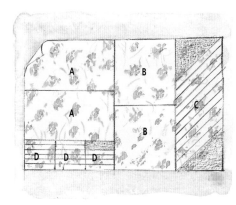

1 Using your measurements, mark the cutting lines on the grain of the fabric and cut out. Mark the letters on each piece.

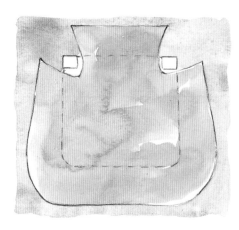

2 Lay paper over the seat, extending down over the upholstery. Mark all around, allowing for the back struts. Mark seam allowances. Cut out and round front corners.

3 Using your measurements for the chair back, make a paper pattern. Round the corners, then mark seam allowances and cut out.

4 Place the patterns on the fabric sections and cut out. From the batting, cut one back and one seat piece along the seam allowances.

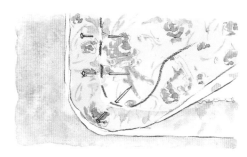

5 Place the two back pieces wrong sides together. Slide the batting in between, then pin and baste.

6 Make six ties for the chair back. Fold each piece of fabric in half lengthwise, right sides together. Pin, then stitch the long side and one short side, with a ⅜ inch seam allowance. Trim, turn right side out and press.

7 To mark the position of the ties, place the back piece on the chair. Mark the first set about 2 inches up from the lower edge and space the other two evenly between this set and the center fold. Pin and baste the ties to the underside, matching the raw edges of the ties to those of the back piece.

8 Join the binding pieces to form two long strips: one for the seat and one for the back.

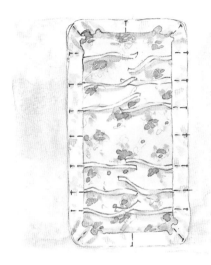

9 Pin the back binding around the edge, right sides together and over the ties. Stitch, taking a ⅜ inch seam allowance. Turn under the binding, then fold over the raw edge to the right side. Pin and stitch through all layers.

10 Make up four pairs of seat ties as in step 6. On one seat section, pin and baste two pairs on both sides of the back strut shaping. Pin both seat pieces right sides together and stitch around the back shaping. Clip into the curved seam allowances, turn right side out and press.

11 Insert the batting as in step 5.

12 Cover the raw edges of the main seat section with the binding, as in step 9.

13 Place the cover on the seat. Holding it firmly in position, fold the front edges into a large dart at each corner. Mark the points where the fabric meets for the ties.

14 Handstitch the seat ties on the underside, as marked, positioning them parallel with the outside edges. When these are tied behind the chair legs, they will hold the cover in position.

We used the same fabric on both sides but you could also use different fabrics for reversible covers.

SEAT CUSHION WITH BOW

Flower and check prints complement one another in this cheery chair cover.

CHECKLIST

Materials

two coordinating closely woven decorator
   fabrics
medium-weight polyester batting
paper for pattern
general sewing equipment   pages 110–11

Techniques

using batting   pages 122–25

Measuring up

To the following measurements, add ⅝ inch
seam allowances:
Seat (fabric and batting) – Measure width
and depth (A). Make a paper pattern for the
shape, see step 2.
Gusset – Measure perimeter of chair seat and
depth (B).
Front skirt – Measure width and multiply
depth by two (C).
Side skirts – Measure width and multiply
depth by two (D).
NOTE: Skirts are double thickness.
Ties – Allow four pieces, ours measure
4 × 28 inches each (E).

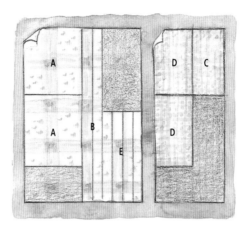

1 Using your measurements, mark the cutting lines on the grain of the fabric and cut out. Mark the letters on each piece.

2 Lay paper over the seat and mark around the outside edges and along the back edge, marking inside the struts. Add the seam allowance and cut out.

3 Place the pattern on the seat fabric sections (A) and cut out. Repeat for the batting. On the seat, gusset (B) and front skirt (C) mark the center front, and center back where appropriate.

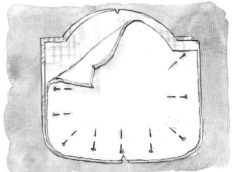

4 Place the two seat pieces with right sides together. Pin the batting to one piece. On the back edge, trim the batting just clear of the seam allowance. Pin and stitch across the back edge between the corners. Trim, snip into the curved seam and turn right side out. Baste the remaining edges together.

5 Place the tie pieces with the right sides together in pairs. Pin and stitch around, stitching diagonally across one short end and leaving the remaining short end open. Clip across the corners of the seam allowance, trim and turn right side out. Press the seams. Pleat the raw edges to fit the width of the gusset and tack to secure. Position each tie piece at the ends of the gusset pieces, laying the ties on the gussets, right sides together and raw edges matching. Pin and baste.

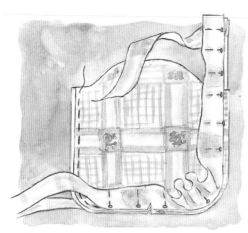

right side out). Pin and stitch across the gusset ends, catching in the ties. Continue, stitching the gusset only, then around the top edge of the gusset also catching in the seat and stitching through all layers. Trim, turn right side out and press. Baste the remaining raw edges of the gussets together.

6 Place the gussets with the right sides together and the ties inside. With the center fronts matching, slide the seat between the gusset pieces towards the lower edge of the gusset (the top edge when turned

7 Fold the front skirt (C) in half lengthwise, right sides together; pin and stitch the side edges only. Trim and turn right side out. Baste the top raw edges together. Repeat for the side skirt pieces (D). Press the seams.

8 Place the skirt pieces on the right side of the gusset, with raw edges matching and the front corners of the skirt evenly positioned. Pin and stitch to the combined gusset edges. Trim and clean finish the raw edges together. Place the cover over the seat and form the ties into a bow at the back.

Depending on your chair, you may need to attach hook and loop tape to the ties and seat back to keep the bow in place.

PLEATED SKIRT COVER

Buttons add interest to this classic cover.

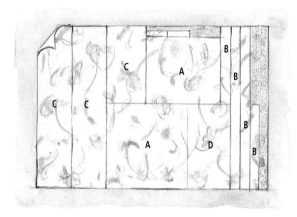

1 Using your measurements, mark the cutting lines on the grain of the fabric and cut out. Mark the letters on the pieces.

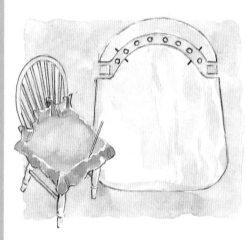

2 Lay a sheet of paper on the seat and mark the contours with pencil. Add the seam allowance, then cut out the pattern. Repeat to make a pattern for the seat outside back. Mark the button and loop positions as shown.

3 Cut out the seat (A) and seat outside back (D) to shape. Repeat for the batting (seat only).

4 Stitch together the short edges of the skirt pieces (C). Press the seams to one side, then clean finish raw edges. Turn under a double hem.

5 Fold the skirt fabric into 3¼ inch box pleats. Adjust the pleats to fit the chair, making sure they fall evenly at the front corners. Pin and baste along the top edge to secure.

6 For the button loops, fold each piece of fabric in half lengthwise. Pin and stitch the long edges. Trim and turn right side out.

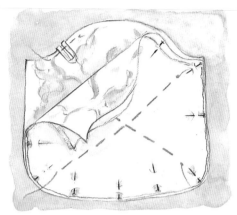

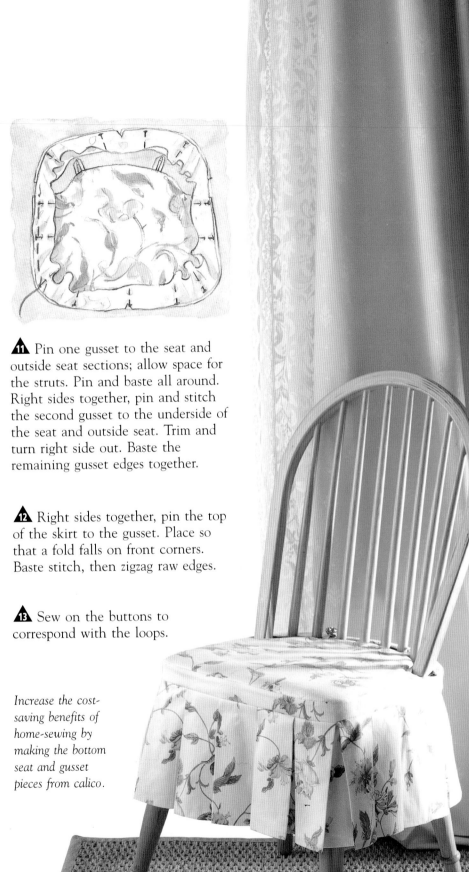

7 Fold each piece into a loop. Pin and tack in place as marked on main seat fabric. Place the main seat pieces, right sides together, with the batting on top. Trim batting clear of back seam allowance, then baste to one seat section. Pin and stitch back edge, then trim and turn right side out. Pin unsewn edges together.

8 Pin and stitch the outside seat sections (D) as in step 7, but leave the back edge open and do not use batting. Trim, turn right side out and pin the back edges together.

9 To keep seams neat, the gusset is made from double thickness fabric. With right sides inside, pin and baste enough gusset pieces (B) together to form a circle. Put on chair to check for a snug fit. Repeat for the second (inner) gusset, then stitch.

10 With right sides together and centers matching, mark the center front and center back of one of the gusset pieces.

11 Pin one gusset to the seat and outside seat sections; allow space for the struts. Pin and baste all around. Right sides together, pin and stitch the second gusset to the underside of the seat and outside seat. Trim and turn right side out. Baste the remaining gusset edges together.

12 Right sides together, pin the top of the skirt to the gusset. Place so that a fold falls on front corners. Baste stitch, then zigzag raw edges.

13 Sew on the buttons to correspond with the loops.

Increase the cost-saving benefits of home-sewing by making the bottom seat and gusset pieces from calico.

FOLDING CHAIR COVER

Give your folding chairs a designer look for summer with this stylish, easy-going cover.

CHECKLIST

Materials

heavyweight cotton decorator fabric	
paper for pattern	
general sewing equipment	pages 110–11

Techniques

patterned fabric	pages 122–25
inverted pleats	pages 120–21

Measuring up

To the following measurements, add ⅝ inch seam allowances:

Seat – Measure width and depth (A), plus 1 inch for ease. Make a paper pattern for the shape, see step 2.

Inside back – Measure width and the depth to the seat (B).

Outside back – Measure the width around the back legs and depth from top of inside back to floor (C) plus hem allowance.

Front skirt – Measure the top width around three sides of the seat plus 12 inches for inverted pleats, and depth plus hem allowance (D).

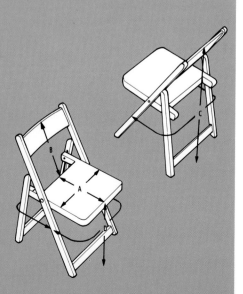

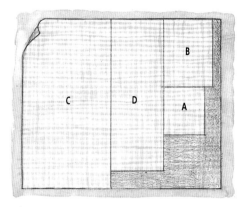

1 Using your measurements, mark the cutting lines on the grain of the fabric and cut out. Mark the letters on each piece.

2 For the shaped seat section, lay paper on the seat and trace around the edges, curving along the inside back edge. Cut out the seat piece (A) using the paper pattern.

3 With a check, you will need to adjust the fabric to ensure that the center line of every piece matches. On the appropriate pieces (back pieces, seat and skirt), notch the seam allowance to mark center points.

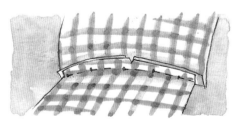

4 Lay the seat (A) and inside back (B) on the chair, wrong sides out. Pin where they meet along the curved line of the inside back edge, matching center notches. Baste, then stitch. Press the seam towards the back.

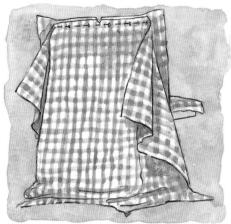

5 Place on the chair, wrong side out. Pin the outside back (C) to the inside back (B) along the top, matching center notches. Following the angle of the chair frame, pin the back and front together at the sides, as far as the seat. The seamline at the top is taken along the top edge of the inside back, so you will need small darts at the top corners of the outside back to allow for the struts.

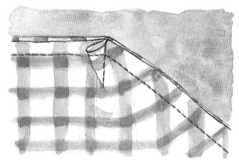

6 Baste and stitch the darts, then trim the seams as far as the seat. Place on the chair wrong side out and pin around the back.

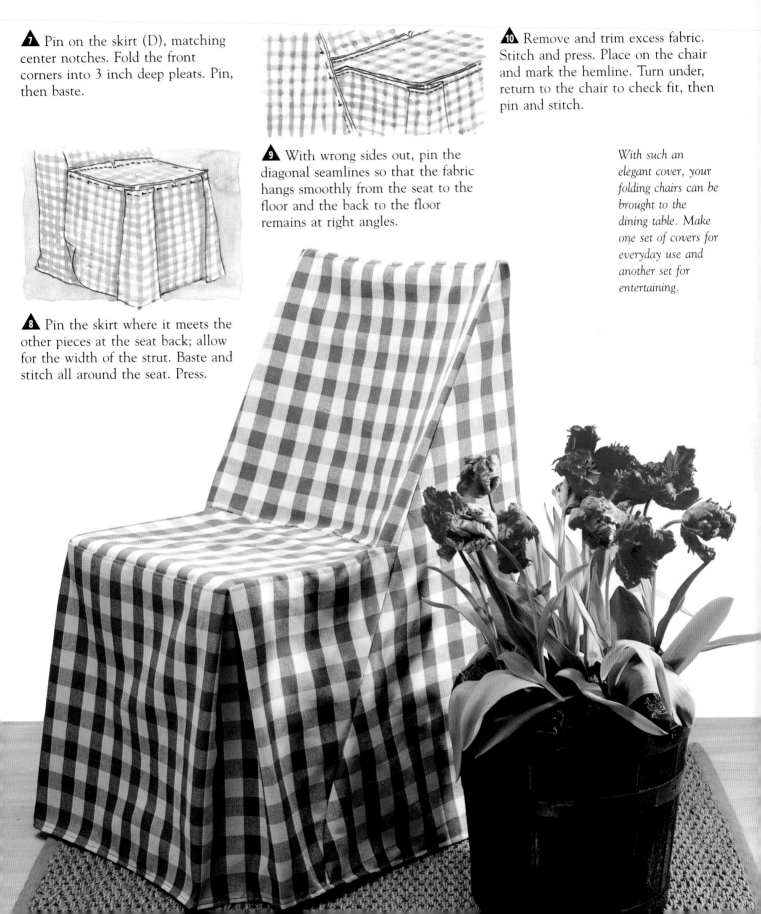

7 Pin on the skirt (D), matching center notches. Fold the front corners into 3 inch deep pleats. Pin, then baste.

8 Pin the skirt where it meets the other pieces at the seat back; allow for the width of the strut. Baste and stitch all around the seat. Press.

9 With wrong sides out, pin the diagonal seamlines so that the fabric hangs smoothly from the seat to the floor and the back to the floor remains at right angles.

10 Remove and trim excess fabric. Stitch and press. Place on the chair and mark the hemline. Turn under, return to the chair to check fit, then pin and stitch.

With such an elegant cover, your folding chairs can be brought to the dining table. Make one set of covers for everyday use and another set for entertaining.

DIRECTOR'S CHAIR COVER

In a child's room or in the garden, this all-season denim cover will transform an ordinary director's chair.

Measuring up

To the following measurements, add ⅝ inch seam allowances:

Inside back – Measure width and depth from inside back edge over the top allowing for the width of the struts (A).

Outside back – Measure width and depth to floor (B).

Seat – Measure width and depth, allowing 1 inch for all around ease (C).

Arms – Measure width and depth from seat over the arm and down to the floor (D).

Front skirt – Measure width and depth (E).

Bows – Allow two squares, ours measure 10 inches, plus two rectangular strips (F).

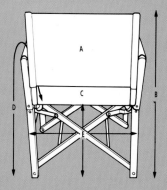

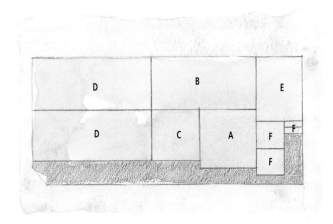

1 Using your measurements, mark the cutting lines on the grain of fabric and cut out. Mark the letters on each piece and clean finish raw edges.

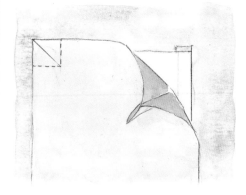

2 On the inside back (A), form darts at the top corners to accommodate the width of the chair struts. Fold the darts, right sides together. Baste and machine stitch. Remove the basting and trim excess.

3 Place the inside back on the chair. Mark the points where the arm rests break into the vertical line, then cut out a narrow rectangle, as shown, to accommodate them.

4 To allow for the canvas chair back bowing when under pressure, add two darts just in from the lower inside back corners. Pin and stitch. Trim and press the dart towards the inside back.

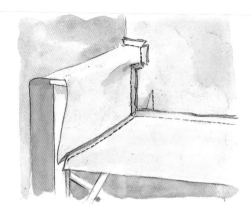

5 Place the inside back and the seat (C) on the chair, wrong sides out and pin and stitch. Trim seam allowances. Pin the arm pieces (D) to the seat sides. Mark, then cut out a rectangle from front edge of arm to match that on the inside back. Stitch the seat to the arms on both sides, then to the inside back, stitching between the rectangles.

6 Bring the outside arm pieces across to meet the front edge of the inside arms. Pin, baste and stitch, curving the angled seam over the front arm rests.

7 With right sides together, pin the outside and inside back together along the top and down the sides, as far as the arm rests. Ease the outside back around the arm rest and continue to pin together the outside back and outside arm pieces. Remove, baste and stitch.

8 Replace the cover, wrong side out and pin the front skirt (E) to the seat and the outside arm pieces. Baste and stitch.

9 Replace the cover and mark the hemline. Turn under a double hem.

10 Clean finish the edges on the bow pieces (F) with narrow hems. Fold in the long edges of the bow strips (F) and glue. Pleat the bows like a fan, place a strip around the middle and stitch to the cover.

As the spirit takes you, your director's chair can be dressed for the part. Here in rugged denim with bows, but diaphanous muslin with dried flowers could be next.

DECK CHAIR

Covering your outdoor furniture is simple and requires a minimum of sewing.

CHECKLIST

Materials

heavyweight deck chair canvas
heavy-duty sewing machine needle and thread
heavy-duty staples and staple gun (or hammer, push pins and upholstery nails)
carpenter's square and ruler
general sewing equipment   pages 110–11

Techniques

machine stitching   pages 114–15

Measuring up

Measure the width between the struts at the bottom and the top; add hem allowances. Lay the chair flat and measure the length, allowing extra to wrap around the top rail for securing the canvas.

1 If your canvas is only slightly wider than the chair frame, turn under a single hem on both long edges to fit.

2 Using the carpenter's square and ruler, check that both ends of the canvas form true right angles. Trim to adjust if necessary. Zigzag short edges to prevent fraying.

3 Position the top edge of the canvas on the underside of the top fixing strut, with the canvas parallel to the edge of the strut. Working outwards from the middle, insert evenly spaced staples.

4 Alternatively, to nail the canvas in place, position it in the same way as before. Hold in place temporarily with one or two push pins, then secure with evenly spaced upholstery nails.

5 Wrap the canvas once around the top strut, smoothing it evenly. Turn the frame over and, pulling the canvas taut, take it around the bottom strut. Staple or nail in position as before.

*Bright, floral striped
fabric will perk up
any patio.*

STAPLES AND NAILS

A staple gun is useful for attaching fabric quickly and effectively to a wooden frame. Warning: always point the gun away from you as the staples can be fired accidentally.

Upholsterer's tacks (nails) come in two varieties: improved tacks which have large heads and fine tacks with smaller heads. Use with an ordinary woodworking or upholsterer's hammer, which has a comparatively heavier head, to tap in the tacks firmly.

Either of these techniques can also be used for permanently attaching fabric to a stool top or chair seat, for example. You can cover the staples or tacks with silk braid or fringed edging, glued with fabric adhesive.

CAPTAIN'S CHAIR

Make two different canvas slings for your chair and you can change them with the seasons.

C H E C K L I S T

Materials

heavyweight deck chair canvas
heavy-duty sewing machine needle and
    thread
carpenter's square and ruler
nylon cord
heavy-duty eyelet kit
general sewing equipment   pages 110–11

Techniques

machine stitching   pages 114–15

Measuring up

Allow one length of fabric. Measure the width between the struts top and bottom; add 2 inches for hem allowances. Measure the length of the back and seat and allow double fabric; add 20 inches for deep hems at the short edges.

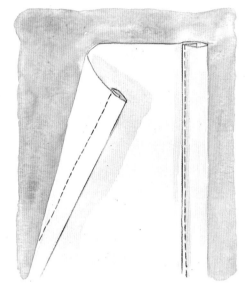

1 With the wrong side facing, make narrow double hems along both long edges and stitch.

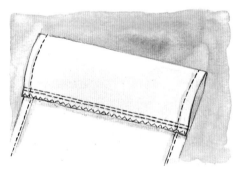

2 Make sure the corners of the two short sides are at right angles to the long sides: trim, if necessary, and zigzag to clean finish. On both short sides, turn under a deep, 5 inch hem to the wrong side. Pin and stitch across the finished edge with a ½ inch seam. Stitch a second row just inside of the first stitching line.

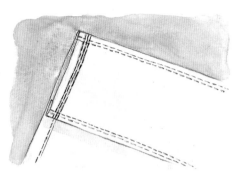

3 Stitch across the folded edge of each end, 1 inch inside the fold. Depending on your fabric, stitch a second line ¼ inch inside the first one, for added strength.

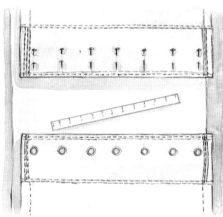

4 On both short sides, mark the position of the seven eyelets evenly outside the double stitching line on the folded edge. Follow the instructions given with the kit to insert the heavy-duty eyelets.

5 Place the cover on the chair, taking it from the top, under the lower back strut, over the front seat rail and back under the lower back strut, so the short ends nearly meet at the outside back.

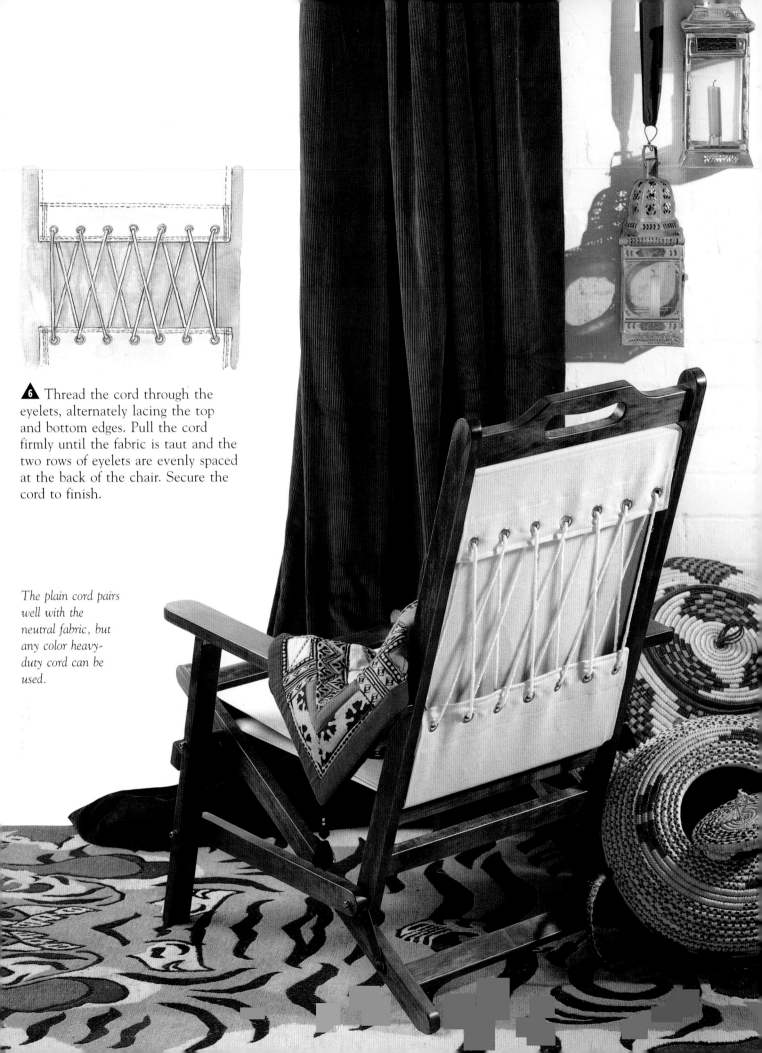

6 Thread the cord through the eyelets, alternately lacing the top and bottom edges. Pull the cord firmly until the fabric is taut and the two rows of eyelets are evenly spaced at the back of the chair. Secure the cord to finish.

The plain cord pairs well with the neutral fabric, but any color heavy-duty cord can be used.

DIRECTOR'S CHAIR

Replacing worn covers will extend the life of these fold-up chairs – useful for extra seating inside or outside the home.

CHECKLIST

Materials

heavyweight deck chair canvas
heavy-duty sewing machine needle and
 thread
heavy-duty staples and staple gun or hammer
 and upholstery nails
carpenter's square and ruler
large eyelet kit
general sewing equipment   pages 110–11

Techniques

machine stitching   pages 114–15

Measuring up

Seat – Measure the width plus 7 inches for hem allowances and wrap around. Measure the depth plus 3 inches for hem allowances (A).
Back – Measure the width plus 7 inches for hems and wrap around. Measure the depth from within the curve of the batten, plus 3 inches for hem allowances (B).

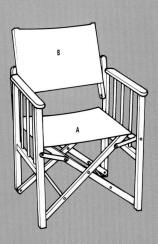

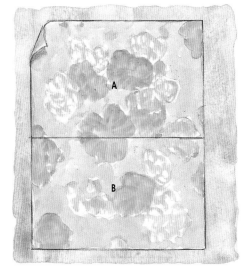

1 Using the old cover as a template or your measurements, mark the cutting lines horizontally on the straight grain of the fabric. If using fabric with a pattern, it should run vertically. Cut out the pieces.

2 On the seat section, zigzag all four raw edges to clean finish. Turn under a single 1 inch hem to the wrong side along the front and back edges and stitch across. Stitch a second line ¼ inch inside the previous stitching.

3 Along each side edge of the seat section, turn under and press a single 1 inch hem to the wrong side of the fabric.

4 Lay the chair on its side and position the side edge of the fabric centrally on the inner underside edge of the seat frame, attaching with only a few staples to check fit. The pressed edge should run parallel with the underside edge of the frame.

5 Working outwards from the center of the chair, nail or staple the seat section in place to the underside of the frame.

6 Turn the chair to the opposite side. In the same way, attach the seat first with two or three staples. Check the fit and adjust if necessary, before nailing or stapling the second side in place.

7 On the back piece, zigzag the raw edges along the top and lower edges. Turn under a single 1 inch hem on each edge and stitch in place with two rows of stitching as before.

8 Zigzag stitch the two side edges. Turn under the side edges with single 1 inch hems and press.

9 To mark the position of the bolt holes on the fabric, wrap the side edges of the fabric around the battens (they will already have been removed from the chair). You will need two holes on either side of the battens. Check that the chair back fits the chair, then working from the wrong side, fix the eyelets in place.

11 Replace the chair back so that the battens are behind the fabric at the back.

MEASURING UP
Instead of measuring, make use of the old cover. Remove the worn cover from the chair and, as you do, make a note of how the individual pieces have been attached. Open out the fabric pieces, unpick any seams and press them flat. Use these to estimate the quantities required for the new cover and, if they are in good shape, save them to be used as pattern pieces. Do not use if the old cover is stretched.

10 Position the fabric edges, right side against the wood, along the rear inside edge of the wooden battens. Working outwards from the middle, staple or nail the fabric to the batten, making sure the eyelets align with the holes in the chair frame.

A new cover will not look as good on an old frame so be sure to sand and paint or varnish your chair before attaching fabric.

BEDROOMS
& BOUDOIRS

Rooms to relax in require adaptable covers and the projects in this chapter are just that, whether your style is formal, rustic or modern. From the clean, classical lines of a daybed with bolster cushions, to a futon with a contemporary look, these covers are designed to look good, night and day.

DAYBED COVER

Bolster cushions and a skirt add elegance to any daybed.

CHECKLIST

Materials

closely woven decorator fabric
pre-shrunk piping cord
zipper for the box cushion: 6 inches
   longer than the back edge
zippers for bolsters: 6 inches shorter
   than the length
general sewing equipment   pages 110–11
2 tassels

Techniques

piping and binding   pages 118–19
inserting zippers   pages 116–17
inverted pleats   pages 120–21

Measuring up

To the following measurements, add ⅝ inch
seam allowances:
Box cushion – Measure length and width (A);
allow for top and bottom pieces.
Front cushion boxing strip – Measure length
from mid-sides and depth (B).
Back cushion boxing strip – Measure length
as for B, and depth plus 1¼ inch zipper seam
allowance (C).
Skirt deck (top panel) – Same as A (D).
Skirt – Measure width from mid-front to
mid-side plus 16 inches per pleat, and depth
plus hem allowance, allow four pieces (E).
Bolsters – Measure the circumference and
width of the main section (F); for the ends,
measure circumference plus the radius (G).
Piping – Allow for bias strips (H).

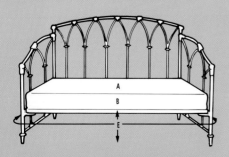

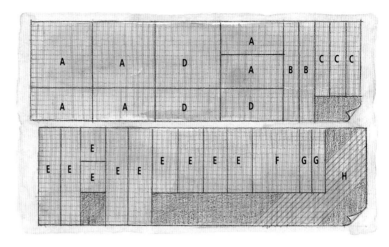

1 Using your measurements, mark the cutting lines on the grain of the fabric and cut out. Mark the letters on each piece.

2 Make up sufficient piping to trim the top and bottom edges of the cushion and the bolsters.

3 To make up the box cushion length, cut one fabric section A in half widthwise. Join the halves to one full section along the short edges, matching any pattern. Repeat for the second cushion side.

4 For the cushion zipper, cut the back gusset (C) in half lengthwise. With right sides together, baste and press the seam open. Place the zipper right side down centrally over the wrong side of the opening. Baste, then stitch on the right side using the zipper foot.

5 Stitch the boxing strip pieces (B and C) along the short edges, leaving ⅝ inch unstitched at each end.

6 Baste piping around the top and bottom edges of the cushion (A). With right sides inside and centers matching, pin and stitch the boxing strip to the top piece on all four sides. Attach the cushion underside in the same way.

7 Snip into the seam allowances at the corners, clean finish the seams and press. Remove basting, open the zipper and turn right side out.

8 To make up the skirt, stitch the pieces (E) along the short edges and press the seams open. Turn under a double hem along the bottom edge.

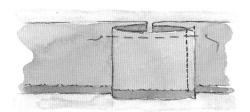

9 Arrange the skirt pleats, placing one at each corner and one centrally at each side. Baste across the top to hold. Press on both sides.

10 Place the deck (D) and skirt right sides together, raw edges and corners matching. Baste, snip into corners at the seam allowance and stitch. Clean finish seams.

11 With right sides together, apply piping to the two circumference edges of the bolster sections (F).

12 To fit the bolster zipper, fold the main section (F) in half, raw edges and right sides together. Baste across the ends, leaving a central opening the length of the zipper. Stitch, then press open. Baste and stitch the zipper in place, see step 4.

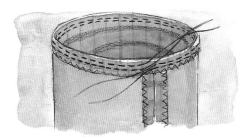

13 On one end piece (G), zigzag the long sides. Stitch the short sides, right sides together, and press the seam open. Repeat for the second end piece. Run two rows of gathering stitches along one turned under edge of each piece.

14 With right sides together, stitch the ends (G) to the main bolster sections.

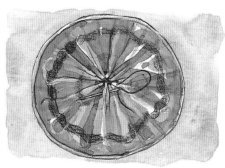

15 Pull up the gathers, bringing the edges together to form a circle. Fasten off securely. Attach tassels to the center of each end, stitching the cord neatly behind the gathers.

To save time and money, skip the back skirt if your daybed is against a wall and make the skirt deck panel from curtain lining or sheets.

HEADBOARD COVER

Coordinate your bedroom
furnishings with a fitted cover
for your headboard, tied in
place with pretty bows.

C H E C K L I S T

Materials

closely woven decorator fabric
paper for pattern
general sewing equipment   pages 110–11

Techniques

machine stitching   pages 114–15

Measuring up

To the following measurements, add $\frac{5}{8}$ inch
for all seam allowances:
Main panels – Measure width and depth (A),
then make a paper pattern for the shape, see
step 2.
Gusset – Measure the depth and length and
add 3 inches at each end for a tuck-in (B).
Ties – Allow four pairs, ours each measure $1\frac{1}{4}$
inches wide by 10 inches long (C).

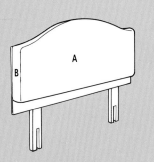

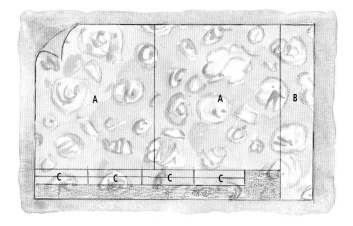

1 Using your measurements, mark
the cutting lines on the grain of the
fabric and cut out. Mark the letters
on each piece.

2 Pin paper to the headboard and
draw around the contour. Add $1\frac{1}{2}$
inches to each side edge for hems
and 7 inches to the bottom edge, for
a tuck-in and hem. Cut out one
fabric section to shape for the back.

3 For the front panel, cut out the
lower corners on the paper pattern as
shown to allow for mitered corners
around the padding, if padded, then
cut out the fabric to shape.

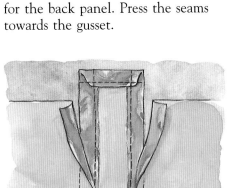

4 With right sides together, pin
the gusset to the front panel, leaving
the outer $1\frac{1}{2}$ inches at either side
unstitched. Baste and stitch. Repeat
for the back panel. Press the seams
towards the gusset.

5 Stitch a double hem on the
short edges of the gusset. Clean
finish the seam allowances by
stitching a single hem and folding in
the corners diagonally.

6 Turn under and stitch a double hem along the side edges of the front and back panels and along the bottom edges.

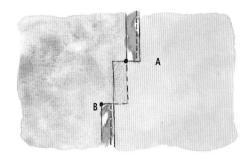

7 On the front panel, clean finish the side edges as far as the cut-in and then clean finish the tuck-in edge below, snipping across the seam allowance at point B. Trim away the shaded area, place points A and B together, right sides inside and stitch to form a mitered corner to accommodate the depth of the headboard.

8 For the ties, fold each piece so the raw edges of the long sides meet in the middle, wrong sides inside. Fold in half lengthwise, then stitch. Alternatively, secure the cover using fabric loops and buttons, or simplify the task by using ribbons in place of the fabric ties.

If your bed is against a wall, use sheeting to make up the back side of the cover, which will cut down on the amount of decorator fabric required.

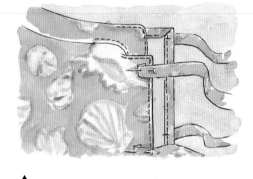

9 Place the cover on the headboard right side out. Position the ties about $\frac{3}{4}$ inch in from the edge. Fold in the ends, then baste and stitch.

DRESSING TABLE COVER

Pretty fabrics, combined with elementary sewing skills, can be used imaginatively to dress up a dressing table.

CHECKLIST

Materials

three coordinating cotton decorator fabrics
standard curtain shirring tape and hooks or
  hook and loop tape
paper for pattern
fabric glue
general sewing equipment   pages 110–11

Techniques

patterned fabric	pages 122–25
ruffles and pleats	pages 120–21
bias strips	pages 118–19

Measuring up

To the following measurements, add ⅝ inch for all seam allowances:

Table top – Measure length and width (A) and make a paper pattern for the shape, see step 2.

Scalloped band – Measure the perimeter and the depth plus hem allowance (B).

Skirt – Measure the perimeter and allow double for gathered fullness on the bias, and the depth (C).

Ruffle – For the width, double the perimeter measurement of the skirt, and measure the depth plus hem allowance (D).

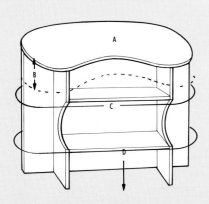

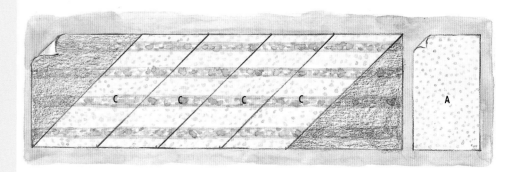

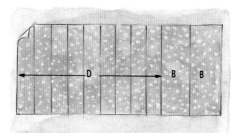

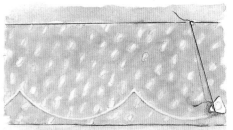

1 Using your measurements, mark the cutting lines for each section on the grain of the fabric and cut out. Mark the letters on each piece.

2 Lay paper over the dressing table top. Mark around the edge, add the seam allowance and cut out. Place the pattern on the table top fabric (A) and cut out.

3 To scallop the edge of the band, lay the fabric section B right side down. Divide evenly into desired scallop widths, then draw in the arcs, using a makeshift compass – a piece of string attached to tailor's chalk. An average scallop is 10 inches wide by 2 inches deep. Mark the seam allowance and hem and cut out. Snip into the seam allowance at the top of each scallop.

4 Following the hem mark, fold under a single turning and press. Work outwards from the middle of each scallop, creating small tucks in the hem where necessary. Secure with fabric glue and leave to dry. Alternatively, stitch the hem.